FRESH
FLOWER
ARRANGING

FRESH
FLOWER
ARRANGING

JERRY ROSE
with LISA SHELKIN

Photography by Tim Lee and Bruce McCandless

HOBBIES &
PASTIMES

A FRIEDMAN GROUP BOOK

This edition published in 1994 by
Magna Books,
Magna Road,
Wigston,
Leicester LE18 4ZH
U.K.

ISBN 1 85422 5472

FRESH FLOWER ARRANGING
A Seasonal Guide to Selection, Design, and Arrangement
was prepared and produced by
Michael Friedman Publishing Group, Inc.
15 West 26th Street
New York, New York 10010

Editor: Kelly Matthews
Art Director: Jeff Batzli
Designer: Tanya Ross-Hughes
Photography Director: Christopher C. Bain

Colour separations by Scantrans Pte. Ltd.
Printed and bound in China by
Leefung-Asco Printers Ltd.

Dedication

For my dad, Lou Rose, who has always lent his help and support and shared his knowledge and love.

Acknowledgments

I would like to extend my sincere appreciation to Kelly Matthews, Karla Olson, and everyone at the Friedman Group for orchestrating this project. My gratitude also goes to Lisa Shelkin, whose writing skills and patience helped shape my ideas into a book.

A special thank-you goes to all those who so graciously allowed us to photograph in their lovely homes: John and Marcia for their kindness; Irwin and Karen for all the laughs; Richard and Betty for their friendship; Bill and Alla Broeksmit for sharing their home; and Michael and Eileen Friedman for giving us a day in their Manhattan apartment.

Thanks also to Tim Lee and Bruce McCandless for their beautiful photographs; Fischer & Page in Manhattan for the freshest of flowers; Michelle Knopman for her never-ending suggestions; Pam Fani for always trying to make it to the next shoot; everyone at Jerry Rose, Inc., for their assistance and backing; and my mom for always asking when the book will be coming out.

And my heartfelt appreciation and thanks goes out to Debra.

Table of Contents

Introduction

I am fortunate that I get to spend my days literally surrounded by dozens and dozens of glorious, delicate, fragrant fresh flowers. This is without a doubt a flower lover's dream, but living in a flower-filled environment doesn't have to be the province of the professional florist alone. You too can bring beautiful flowers into your day-to-day life by creating arrangements of fresh-cut blooms each week at home. Here, in this book, I have created fifty-two original flower designs—one for every week of the year—to serve as both guides and inspiration for a year brimming with spectacular flowers.

My arrangements were inspired by the colors, scents, shapes, and textures of the seasons. I have used only the freshest materials, elements that follow the natural progression of the months and can be purchased locally or harvested from your own garden or yard. The list of elements included with each arrangement will serve as a clear-cut guide for selecting flowers, but with the special attention I have paid to the variety of natural materials available throughout the year, my hope is to provide an impetus for both the novice and expert arranger to experiment. Try working not only with different flower colors and shapes, but also with such surprising ingredients as produce, branches, moss, and grass.

As you experiment, keep in mind that there is no such thing as a perfect arrangement. Move the stems about, positioning them into an arrangement that you personally find pleasing. With the help of my guidelines and suggestions, you will discover your own preferences and develop your own arranging style. By following your instincts, flower arranging can be a relaxing experience, a type of therapy that allows you to use your creativity and blocks everything else out of your mind.

As your familiarity with flowers and confidence in arranging them grows, always remember to let the flowers, especially their colors, do the work. I recommend working with a palette of your favorite colors and using them to their full advantage. Think of yourself as an artist and the flowers as brushstrokes. By combining different colors, you can evoke images that are bold and stunning or calm and tranquil. The only difference between a painter and a floral designer is that the flowers are not permanent; they are only for the moment.

Flower arrangements are most appealing when they've been given a special, personal touch. Anyone can purchase a bunch of tulips and place them in a vase, but notice the difference when you give them some additional attention. Enjoy the time that you spend each week experimenting and designing with flowers. It can easily become a treasured weekly activity—one that you will want to continue for years to come.

Spring

An exuberant assortment of springtime specials wait to be conditioned, cut, arranged, and enjoyed. Some of this season's favorites include (counterclockwise from top left) green viburnum, purple lilacs, forsythia, blue grape hyacinths, pink hyacinths, mini tulips, white sweet peas, Ad Rem tulips, purple hyacinths, white grape hyacinths, smilax vines, grape hyacinths, parrot tulips, Fire 'n Ice roses, lily-of-the-valley, daffodils, and paper whites.

Springtime Centerpiece

Celebrate the first days of spring by creating a spectacular centerpiece of lilacs, astilbe, forsythia, viburnum, and Ad Rem, Gudoshnik, and pencil tulips for the dining room table. Lush green smilax placed around an old Staffordshire soup tureen serves as a natural setting, helping to warm up an otherwise formal room. Fully opened red roses scattered in small glass bud vases throughout the smilax highlight the arrangement.

ELEMENTS

10 Ad Rem tulips

6 Gudoshnik tulips

6 pink pencil tulips

15 stems of purple lilac

6 stems of forsythia

25 green viburnum

12 stems of astilbe

12 Fire 'n Ice roses

10 smilax vines

Fresh Spanish moss, as needed

1 16-inch soup tureen

12 glass bud vases

2 1/2 blocks of oasis

DIRECTIONS

Cut and fit the wet oasis into the container. Begin arranging by placing the larger woody stems of forsythia and lilac into the oasis, creating a framework for the arrangement. Next, place the green viburnum, positioning half of the stems toward the lower part of the design (the full, round head of the viburnum can be used to hide the lip of the receptacle). Choose the most beautiful tulips, and place them in the center and at the sides of the arrangement, where they can most easily be seen. Continue to place the tulips, astilbe, and any extra forsythia or lilac while checking that there is a balance of flowers on all sides. Fill in any openings with Spanish moss. Add water. Once the arrangement has been moved to the table, surround it with smilax, and add the red roses in bud vases as accents.

TRADE SECRET

Sold by the bag, smilax can be purchased a few days before an event if it is kept moist and refrigerated. This beautiful greenery will then stay fresh for the duration of a party without the need of any further watering.

A Gathering of Bouquets

Spring is the season to bring freshly cut flowers inside to savor their beauty and enticing aromas. Here, in this bedroom, the scents emanating from the paper whites and grape hyacinths flood the room, and the mini tulips, sweet peas, and forsythia add touches of brilliant color and an array of textures. Smilax is used to dress the white wicker serving cart.

ELEMENTS

75 paper whites

50 sweet peas

40 to 50 purple grape hyacinths

75 mini tulips

1 branch of forsythia

10 smilax vines

Raffia, as needed

5 containers of various sizes and heights

DIRECTIONS

Condition and cut flowers, placing them into their selected vases. Spread plenty of smilax over the chosen surface, creating a luxurious green carpet. Mist and inhale.

TRADE SECRET

Other flowers to use for their glorious fragrance are lilies, lily-of-the-valley, roses, lilacs, jasmine, and wallflowers.

Mantelpiece in Bloom

To get a head start on the magic that bursts forth in spring, bring in cuttings from the yard before they bloom, and keep a close watch as the combination of heat, light, and water forces them to open early. Here, on this nineteenth-century Italianate mantel, branches from a magnolia tree make an early April appearance. When cutting branches, consider ceiling height. Because the ceilings in this room are twelve feet high, the branches were cut to measure four to six feet in length. Purple and pink hyacinths sit stoutly in crystal bud vases and antique cruets, adding texture and brightness. Vines of smilax drape effortlessly across the mantel shelf, blending the various colors.

TRADE SECRET

Branches of almost all outdoor flowering trees and shrubs can be brought inside and forced to bloom. From dogwood, decorative cherry, forsythia, rhododendron, decorative crab apple, and magnolia in spring to holly, white pine, flat cedar, Bayberry, and spruce in winter, these branches can be gathered right in your own backyard. Plunge them into tepid water and put them in a sunny window, and you will experience an early spring.

ELEMENTS

6 magnolia branches

10 pink/purple hyacinths

10 smilax vines

7 bud vases

2 16-inch urns or vases

DIRECTIONS

Cut magnolia or other flowering branches from trees with pruning shears after the buds have developed (for magnolia, wait until the flower has shown). If the stems are woody, smash the bottoms with a hammer, which will allow them to drink more water. Bring the stems indoors, and immediately plunge them into tepid water. Flowering should begin in one to four weeks, with the open magnolia blooms lasting for two weeks. Place ample amounts of smilax on the mantel, allowing it to hang gracefully off both sides. Cut hyacinths low so that the heads hug the tops of the vases. Set them on the mantel.

Popped Tulips

Tulips always appear to be searching for something, and when their blooms are wide open, they take on a personality all their own. In this elegant silver vase, Gudoshnik tulips are spotlighted. The few stems of forsythia add height and scale, and their bright yellow color brings out the yellow streaks in the wandering tulips.

ELEMENTS

6 red and yellow Gudoshnik tulips

3 branches of forsythia

1 12-inch vase

DIRECTIONS

Condition and cut the tulips, removing any damaged leaves. Condition the forsythia, cutting it into lengths twice the height of the container. Randomly add the tulips; they should be about half the height of the forsythia. As the tulips bend and roam, they will add additional charm.

TRADE SECRET

Force tulips and other bulbs to bloom indoors in the winter by potting and watering the bulbs and then placing them in a cool, dark location for eight to twelve weeks. When the plants begin to break through the dirt, move them to a lighter location. After one week or when the tulips have reached approximately six inches in height, move them to a cool spot in direct sunlight. Continue to water and the bulbs will come into full bloom.

Decorative Daffodils

Although a bathroom is frequented by guests, it is often overlooked when flowers are considered. Why not give the bathroom a lift with the beauty and warmth of a floral bouquet? Here, daffodils and mini tulips cut fresh from the garden dress up an otherwise empty corner. A terra-cotta pot and ceramic pitcher continue the earthy outdoor theme.

TRADE SECRET

Always keep fresh Spanish moss or dampened sheet moss on hand when creating arrangements. After all the flowers have been set in place, the moss can be used to surround the flower stems. This will add texture, depth, and support.

ELEMENTS

40 daffodils

20 mini tulips

Fresh Spanish moss, as needed

Plastic liner, as needed

1 8-inch container

1 4-inch pitcher

DIRECTIONS

Fit the container with a plastic liner if using terra-cotta (terra-cotta is too porous to hold water on its own) and fill with water. If the container is going to be placed in a corner, cut and place the daffodils as they might grow in the wild. This can be achieved by placing a few daffodils that have been cut very short in the front part of the container. Be generous; place as many flowers as possible into the container without damaging the stems. Pack Spanish moss around the stems for support. Cut the mini tulips so they are twice the height of the pitcher, and place them so some will stray in different directions, which will soften and balance the upright position of the daffodils.

In the Study With Tea

Transform a quiet study into a glorious spring garden in full bloom. Here, as an overabundance of peach parrot tulips twist and bend in search of sunlight, their shape and rich color contrast nicely with the stiff form of the purple lilacs. Experimenting with unusual mixtures of colors such as these can create exciting compositions. Remember, it's not necessary to match the flowers to a room's color scheme. Arrangements will stand out from the furnishings when the flowers are from a contrasting or complementary palette.

ELEMENTS

15 peach parrot tulips

25 to 30 stems of purple lilac

2 blocks of oasis

1 10-inch fruit bowl

DIRECTIONS

Cut blocks of wet oasis and fit them into the container. Cut and condition lilac branches, and place most of the stems into the oasis, distributing them evenly and assessing the arrangement from all angles. Next, add the tulips in a random pattern. Allow space between them as they will move, open, and grow once watered. Fill in any open spaces with the last few lilac branches, cutting them short and placing them carefully into any dark holes in the arrangement. Add water.

TRADE SECRET

When using oasis to arrange bulbs such as tulips or ranunculus blooms, be sure to refill the container with water often. The oasis has a tendency to dehydrate the water-filled blooms.

24

A Grouping of Grape Hyacinths

A simple and delicate arrangement can easily make a bold statement. This grouping of tiny white grape hyacinths is not lost in this large room because they command attention sitting up high on an antique tole occasional table. The unexpected use of the inkwell as a container and the delightful addition of an opened tulip attract the eye to this still-life setting.

ELEMENTS

25 white grape hyacinths

1 Ad Rem tulip

3 short containers

DIRECTIONS

Cut the hyacinth stems so the blooms will be close to the tops of the containers, and remove leaves as needed. Fill each container to capacity, being careful not to break the flowers. Cut the stem of the tulip very short. Try grouping the containers under a spotlight for a theatrical effect.

TRADE SECRET

Don't be afraid to cut your flower stems short. If a stem breaks, cut it off near the bloom and float the flower in a dish of water. A single bud displayed in this manner is quite engaging.

Rainbow of Tulips

Making an impressive appearance in early spring, tulips burst forth in a medley of shapes and a profusion of colors. Combining a mélange of tulip forms and colors, such as the explosion of black parrot, Angelique, Bellona, and peach tulips shown here, produces an eclectic arrangement, one that is harmonious and uniform while at the same time irregular and daring.

ELEMENTS

15 black parrot tulips

10 Bellona tulips

10 peach tulips

12 Angelique tulips

1 10-inch tulip bowl

DIRECTIONS

Fill the container with water. Cut the tulips on an angle with a sharp knife. Remove any damaged leaves that will fall below the water line, and place the stems into the container, trying to separate the different varieties. Allow some of the tulips to hang down and stray in different directions, as they might in the garden.

TRADE SECRET

Do not fill a container to the top with water when making an arrangement with tulips. The tulip stems already hold water, and if the water level is too high, they will not last as long and will drown.

Child's Delight

Flowers placed in unexpected nooks and corners will always bring a smile. Here, in a child's room, Madeline and her friend Linnea take a break from an afternoon of doll-playing to rest comfortably amid a cheerful combination of pink and yellow ranunculus mixed with grape hyacinths. Sitting pertly in a bright red and white Russian porcelain tea set, these arrangements add to the room's playfulness. Note, however, that this grouping has been placed on a mantel well out of reach of inquisitive hands.

ELEMENTS

15 yellow ranunculus

18 pink/coral ranunculus

18 purple grape hyacinths

Sheet moss, as needed

1 block of oasis

1 tea cup

1 4-inch bowl

DIRECTIONS

Cut the wet oasis and fit the blocks snugly into the containers. Remove the excess stems and buds from the ranunculus. Starting at the center and using the tallest and most beautiful blooms, place both the pink and yellow flowers in the oasis. Continue to place the ranunculus in a circular pattern, varying the height at the same time. Cut some of the flowers very short so they are just above the edge of the containers. Next, place grape hyacinths throughout the arrangement in the same fashion, making sure that they have been evenly distributed. Fill any openings with ranunculus foliage, and tuck in sheet moss.

Azaleas in Bloom

Here, sun-kissed clusters of hot-house pink azaleas, dark blue Bellamosa delphinium, feathery astilbe, and peach and pink yarrow perch center stage in aluminum baskets, adding to the springtime spirit of this glorious warm-weather haven.

ELEMENTS

30 Bellamosa delphinium

1 hot-house azalea plant, in full bloom

15 stems of astilbe

12 yarrow

2 6- to 10-inch baskets

2 blocks of oasis

2 plastic liners

DIRECTIONS

Fit the baskets with plastic liners. Cut and divide the wet oasis between the two baskets, and place the blocks inside so that each sits slightly higher than the rim. Cut and clean excess leaves from the azalea and place the conditioned flower stems into the oasis, distributing them throughout the baskets. Allow the bloom-covered branches to trail playfully down the sides of the containers. Trim the delphiniums so that they are twice the height of the containers and place them into the oasis. Cut some delphiniums short and use them to fill in where needed. Insert the astilbe. Lastly, tuck in the yarrow as an accent.

TRADE SECRET

An easy way to revive a wilted azalea plant is to submerge the pot under water for a few minutes. The flowers should come back to life after a short period of time.

Pink Profusion

A gold-leaf mirror and an antique quail-egg hutch at the end of a long hall-way combine to make the perfect setting for an irresistible burst of pink blooms. With a bed of breezy pink astilbe serving as a light base for fanciful pink ranunculus, this unexpected color combination of pink on pink produces a bold display.

ELEMENTS

50 stems of astilbe

70 ranunculus

1 low bowl or dish

1 block of oasis

DIRECTIONS

Place the wet oasis horizontally into the container. Condition and cut the astilbe short, so that the flowers will rest close to the oasis block. Insert the astilbe into the block toward the front of the container, allowing some to hang in a downward direction. Cut and insert the ranunculus into the central portion of the block. Experiment with varying flower heights, allowing them to wander in different directions throughout the arrangement.

35

Romantic Peonies

Sweet-smelling perennials that will flourish and bloom in a garden year after year, peonies produce showy camellia-like flowers. Evoking scenes of charming country gardens, peonies add a touch of romance to an arrangement. Here, pink and white peonies arranged in a Chippendale planter are complemented by bridal veil, tuberoses, and Doris Ryker roses, bringing an intimate atmosphere into the room.

ELEMENTS

4 pink peonies

3 white peonies

8 Doris Ryker roses

7 tuberoses

8 stems of bridal veil

1 12-inch container

2 blocks of oasis

1 plastic liner

Sheet moss, as needed

DIRECTIONS

Line the container with damp sheet moss. Next, slip in the plastic liner, and fit with wet blocks of oasis. Insert three-quarters of the bridal veil into the outer edges of the oasis, allowing it to spill downward. Place the peonies in the center as the focal point of the arrangement. Insert tuberoses for height, and fill in with Doris Ryker roses and the rest of the bridal veil. Tuck in sheet moss.

TRADE SECRET

The best time to pick flowers from your garden is either early in the morning or in the evening after the sun has gone down. Flowers picked in the heat of the day are likely to wilt.

Wedding-Day Topiary

A work of art, this topiary filled with soft pinks, peaches, and whites makes the perfect wedding centerpiece. A bed of ivy and yards of pink satin ribbon cradling votive candles add to the romantic English garden effect.

TRADE SECRET

A topiary makes a fanciful embellishment appropriate for any special occasion. A simple and quick way to create a topiary-like effect is to tuck freshly cut roses or other hearty blooms in among the greenery of such plants as ivy or boxwood.

ELEMENTS

75 Osiana, Livia, and Doris Ryker roses

15 white peonies

10 stems of bridal veil

15 viburnum

15 stems of astilbe

5 pots of variegated and needlepoint English ivy

10 yards of pink satin ribbon

4 votive candles in ivy bowls

1 12-inch azalea pot

1 36-inch birch branch

2 24-inch wooden dowels

4 blocks of oasis, covered in chicken wire

Plaster of paris

1 8-inch sheet of green Styrofoam

Floral tape, as needed

Sheet moss, as needed

DIRECTIONS

Fit the Styrofoam sheet into the bottom of the azalea pot and secure the birch branch in place. Fill the pot half full with plaster of paris, and allow it to set overnight. Drill two holes, side-by-side, approximately six inches down the length of the branch, so that when the dowels are placed in the holes, they will cross each other. Place the dowels through the drilled holes so they are positioned equally on either side of the branch. Next, place the wet oasis bricks on top of the branch and secure with floral tape. Beginning with the peonies, clean and place them evenly throughout the form, including underneath and on the top, creating a rounded shape. Clean and cut the roses, and begin placing them throughout the oasis. The flowers should extend between ten and sixteen inches from the oasis. Next, insert the bridal veil, viburnum, and astilbe, turning the topiary to make certain that the colors and shapes are being evenly distributed on all sides, including the top and the bottom. Continue working until most of the flowers have been placed. Fill any openings with shorter roses and shorter stems of viburnum. Place the pots of ivy on top of the plaster of paris in the container, and fill in any openings with moss. Wrap the pink ribbon around the necks of the ivy bowls, creating a cradle. The ribbon should be approximately twenty-four to thirty-six inches in length. When finished, hang the bowls from the dowels.

Summer

Rich and exotic shades and shapes reach dizzying heights in summer, offering grand and glorious opportunities for floral designs. Awaiting a touch of creativity, flair, and panache are the season's best offerings (counterclockwise from lower right): potted blue hydrangea, Merella roses, pink astilbe, potted mandevilla, Bellamosa delphinium, pink spray garden roses, peach Osiana roses, peach and pink yarrow, pink phlox, purple campanula, potted mandevilla, pink spray garden roses, potted geraniums, spirea, and English ivy plants.

Kitchen Cheer

Nothing cheers a morning quite like radiant blue delphiniums and miniature dahlias nestled in the kitchen corner. This arrangement will last for days, welcoming many mornings and easing any tasks in the kitchen.

ELEMENTS

4 delphiniums

8 miniature dahlias

1 8-inch clay pot

1 block of oasis

1 plastic liner

Sheet moss, as needed

DIRECTIONS

Fit the clay pot with a plastic liner and insert the wet oasis. Fill the container with water. Cut the delphiniums to the same height, three times the height of the container. Next, insert the delphinium stems into the oasis toward the back of the container. Cut the dahlias so that some will be twice as high as the container and others will hug the edge. Insert the dahlias. Tuck sheet moss around the bottom edges of the arrangement.

TRADE SECRET

An arrangement displayed in a simple terra-cotta pot provides any room with a rustic, country ambiance. The most attractive containers have been aged or weathered and can be found at estate sales or flea markets. A reliable alternative is to paint a new terra-cotta pot with yogurt or buttermilk and set it in a cool, damp spot or bake it in the sun. In a few days, it will be covered in a green mold, giving it an aged appearance. These porous pots can also be painted with oil-based paints for a more artful approach.

Summery Snaps

A treasured garden flower, snapdragons have been hybridized for decades, creating a wide range of colors and astounding height. They are available in shades running the gamut from white to yellow, pink, dark red, and even orange. There are many bicolors and bitones as well. Here, a ceramic water pitcher shows off the tall flowering spikes of these sun-loving biennials.

ELEMENTS

100 white, pink, and burgundy

snapdragons

1 12-inch pitcher

DIRECTIONS

Fill the container with water. Clean all the foliage from the stems or the snapdragons will wilt. Cut approximately half of the flowers so that they are at least twice the height of the pitcher, and place them in the container. Cut some stems so the blooms begin just above the lip of the container; others should vary in height below the tallest stems. This arrangement should be created so that it can be viewed from all sides.

TRADE SECRET

Take advantage of all the gardening catalogs you receive at this time of year, and order some bulbs; they will arrive just in time to plant in the autumn. Bulbs also make great gifts. Why not send for naturalized giant daffodils or miniature border tulips that would work in any bed or border or along a walkway or path?

Splendid Sweet Peas

Intermingling the various hues of one particular flower creates a simple yet compelling arrangement any time of the year. Here, a vibrant palette of deep purple, lavender, pink, and fuchsia sweet peas explodes in a gold and copper planter. The deep purple adds visual punch to the centerpiece.

ELEMENTS

50 purple sweet peas

50 lavender sweet peas

50 pink sweet peas

10 fuchsia sweet peas

1 14-inch planter

2 blocks of oasis

2 blocks of Styrofoam

1 plastic liner

DIRECTIONS

Cut and place the Styrofoam blocks into the bottom of the container for height. Set the plastic liner on top, and cut and position the wet oasis on top of the liner. Place the sweet peas into the oasis, taking advantage of the abundant and diverse shades of these flowers by spreading their colors throughout the arrangement. Add water.

Bedroom Designs

Welcome weekend guests to their quarters at a cool summer retreat with an inviting display of brightly colored sunflowers. Used here as vivid accents to punctuate crisp white linens, these majestic flowers have also been gathered more traditionally in a bouquet that graces this tranquil scene. After guests have departed, the flowers can still be enjoyed by drying and using them in clusters as decorations throughout the home.

ELEMENTS

20 sunflowers

1 12-inch ceramic vase

TRADE SECRET

Harvest your own sunflower seeds by cutting and drying mature sunflower heads after the petals have dropped off and the seeds have matured. For a delicious snack, coat the seeds with egg whites, butter, or olive oil, place them on a cookie sheet, and bake them in a 300°F oven for ten to twenty minutes (or until crisp), turning frequently to avoid burning.

DIRECTIONS

Cut five large and four smaller sunflower stems down to the neck and place them on bed linens as you would decorative pillows. Fill the vase with water. Cut and clean eleven flowers, and insert them one by one into the vase so that their faces will be directed out toward the room.

Artful Accents

Strength isn't necessarily in numbers. This distinctive grouping of Merella roses and purple and hot pink sweet peas makes a dramatic, bold statement using very few blooms. The arresting, brightly colored combination becomes an attention-grabber when placed in silver vases of different shapes.

ELEMENTS

14 Merella roses

30 hot pink sweet peas

30 purple sweet peas

5 vases in various shapes

DIRECTIONS

Fill containers with water, and condition and clean roses. Cut the roses to varying heights (some can sit just above the lip of the container, others can be twice that height) and place into the vases. Cut and position sweet peas in containers. Some should be placed for height and others used as color accents. Make sure that all the flower stems are immersed in the water.

TRADE SECRET

When purchasing flowers at a florist's shop or a market, squeeze the base of the flower head to make sure it is firm. This will ensure that the blooms are fresh. Also, check the stems and leaves for mold or discoloration.

A Poolful of Blooms

These garden roses are dramatically spotlighted resting on a built-in table in the center of a whirlpool. These glorious flowers beckon anyone still poolside to come in for a refreshing dip.

ELEMENTS

30 orange garden roses

1 10-inch glass container

DIRECTIONS

Fill the container with water. Clean and condition the roses. Place each rose into the container one by one, arranging the flowers in a loose, rounded bouquet.

TRADE SECRET

To create a handheld bouquet, select and condition the materials ahead of time. Start with one large flower, such as a rose, and add to it with such fillers as railroad annie, solidago, Monte Casino, or some greenery while continuing to hold the arrangement in one hand. Next, add more of the larger flowers, always keeping the stems at an angle and turning it to see that it is even on all sides. Alternate the larger flowers with filler. As the bouquet grows in size, begin to place the smaller stems at the outer edges. Include ivy for a final touch. Tie with raffia, string, or ribbons.

Summer Blue and Yellow

Blue puffs of hydrangea soften the imposing forms of yellow sunflowers in this sun-drenched study in the city on a summer afternoon. The vivid colors of these fresh flowers evoke memories of days spent at the beach strolling along the water underneath a cloudless sky and the ubiquitous sun. The overall effect can be intoxicating.

ELEMENTS

18 sunflowers

45 stems of blue hydrangea

1 18-inch natural wood flower box

2 blocks of oasis

Floral tape, as needed

1 plastic liner

DIRECTIONS

Insert the plastic liner into the wood box, and cut and fit the wet oasis into the lined container. Tape the oasis into the box to secure it and help support the height and weight of the oversize blooms. Cut the sunflowers to varying heights, leaving some tall while cutting others in half or close to the head. Clean off the excess or damaged leaves, and insert the sunflowers into the oasis. Condition the hydrangea by splitting and scraping the woody stems. Insert and tuck the hydrangea into the arrangement to form a pillow-like foundation for the sunflowers.

TRADE SECRET

Give a summer table setting a special touch by using flower stems as napkin rings. Take two or three stems of baby's breath, daisies, safflowers, or any other flower with a long, thin stem, and cluster the blooms together. Twist the stems around each other, and knot them loosely around a folded napkin.

Roses Bathed in Sunlight

Drenched in the reflected light of a midsummer afternoon, this vision of splendid peach and pink roses delivers an elegant impression. The juxtaposition of the two arrangements makes the display twice as spectacular, doubling this treat for the eyes. Yarrow and English ivy play up the natural, less feminine side of this sublime silhouette.

ELEMENTS

25 small pink roses

20 Osiana peach roses

30 stems of yarrow

1 English ivy plant

2 8-inch square wood crates

4 blocks of oasis

2 plastic liners

DIRECTIONS

Condition and clean the roses a few days ahead of time in order to show them at their fullest. Line the crates with plastic, and cut and fit oasis blocks inside, allowing them to sit a few inches above the edges of the containers. Cut ivy stems from the base of the plant and insert them evenly into the sides of the oasis, placing them so they will spill out and drape over the sides of the crates. Cut and place the roses into the oasis on an angle, distributing them evenly throughout the arrangement. Insert yarrow and any remaining ivy. Add water and mist.

TRADE SECRET

When using ivy, it is best to use cuttings from potted plants. Not only is this cost-efficient, but the arrangement will also look fresher and last longer.

Clouds of Hydrangea

The soft round heads of hydrangea make an effective canvas for creating floral sculpture. On this front step, the mixed hues of strawflowers punctuate the bed of light and dark pink hydrangea.

TRADE SECRET

It is easy to create a dried-flower arrangement using hydrangea. Try combining fresh hydrangea with other flowers that are ideal for drying, such as yarrow, strawflowers, and statice. After cleaning all the leaves from the stems, place the flowers into a low basket without water. In one month's time, you will have a delicate, everlasting bouquet.

ELEMENTS

25 light and dark pink hydrangeas

30 yellow, orange, and pink
*   strawflowers*

1 10-inch container

2 blocks of oasis

DIRECTIONS

Cut and fit the wet oasis into the container. Condition the hydrangea. Cut some of the stems short, and begin to place them into the oasis close to the edge of the container. Leave the rest of the hydrangea taller, approximately one and a half times the height of the container, and place them toward the center of the oasis. Clean, cut, and place the strawflowers into the oasis, evenly distributing the flowers throughout the bed of hydrangea. Tuck in some short strawflowers for depth. Be certain to turn the arrangement as the flowers are being placed to create a bouquet that can be viewed from all sides. Fill the container with water and mist.

Dinnertime Dahlias

Available in a wide variety of colors, dahlias can grow up to six feet tall. With blooms ranging in size from two to ten inches wide, these Mexican beauties are splendid when grouped by themselves; their quilled shape does not always mix well with other flowers. Summer greens such as hardy ferns or grasses combine well with dahlias, as do the caladium leaves and viburnum berries shown here.

ELEMENTS

30 dahlias in various colors

3 branches of viburnum berries

10 caladium leaves

2 blocks of oasis

1 cake plate

1 plastic liner

DIRECTIONS

Place the plastic liner fitted with wet oasis blocks onto the cake plate. Cut and insert dahlias around all sides of the oasis to form a rounded shape. The flowers on the bottom should be cut short so they will rest close to the oasis, keeping the ones on top approximately twice the height of the cake plate. Cut viburnum branches into six-inch pieces to act as a natural base, and insert to fill in any openings. The caladium leaves should be placed in central points throughout the arrangement.

Sun-Kissed Sunflowers

Extend the joys of summer by setting out large bunches of resplendent sunflowers, one of the last summer flowers to fade. Fill oversize pots, urns, jugs, and planters with these colorful, statuesque blooms, and place them out on the porch, on the deck, or along a stone path, or arrange groupings on your front steps to extend visitors a warm country welcome.

ELEMENTS

8 sunflowers

4 branches of viburnum berries

1 oversize water pitcher

DIRECTIONS

Fill the container with water. Cut and remove excess leaves from the sunflowers, and insert them into the container. Cut branches of viburnum at various heights and insert to add depth.

TRADE SECRET

In the middle of summer, move arrangements to a cool spot overnight. This will keep the flowers fresher.

Roses By the Basket

A country basket made of natural birch branches moves uptown when a bouquet of sophisticated roses is tucked inside. This container gracefully makes the transition from a more rustic setting and now sits comfortably in a formal environment flanked by candelabras.

ELEMENTS

50 white roses

1 10-inch basket

1 block of oasis

1 plastic liner

Sheet moss, as needed

DIRECTIONS

Line the basket with sheet moss and fit with the plastic liner. Cut and place the wet oasis into the bottom of the basket. Clean and condition the roses. (If this arrangement is being created for a party, allow the roses to sit in buckets of tepid water for a few days before the event, changing the water each day.) Cut and begin to place the roses into the oasis. Some should be cut short and placed close to the edge of the container while those destined for the center should be cut to one and a half times the height of the basket. Turn the arrangement as the roses are being placed to ensure that the bouquet can be viewed from all sides. Continue to place the flowers until the basket is full. When complete, the shape should have a natural unevenness.

Indian Summer

The fuzzy rippled heads of the celosia, or cockscomb, flower make an unusual addition to any floral bouquet. Pictured here with magenta and pink sedum, this eccentric flower completes a picture-perfect arrangement in an antique tin teapot. Keep in mind that this arrangement will also work well in a kitchen or in an informal dining room.

ELEMENTS

6 cockscomb stems

8 magenta and pink sedum

1 teapot or pitcher

DIRECTIONS

Fill the container with water. Cut and insert the cockscomb so that the blooms sit six to eight inches above the rim of the teapot. Cut and place the sedum to separate the cockscomb.

TRADE SECRET

Cockscomb can be dried for use in bouquets during the winter by hanging the cut stems upside down in a well-ventilated spot. Make sure to gather the stems as soon as they bloom.

CHAPTER THREE

Autumn

As the long hot days of summer begin to wane and the weather turns cooler and crisper, nature presents a whole new range of forms, textures, and fragrances perfect for incorporating into flower arrangements. Here is a collection of seasonal ingredients to try this autumn. Counterclockwise from bottom right: calendula, blue thistle, kangaroo paw, blue monkshood, red rover daisies, slootkantia, pink yarrow, orange Sensation roses, yellow Golden Fantasie roses, eucalyptus, yellow roses, miniature calla lilies, railroad annie, yellow solidago, orange safflowers, copper beech branches, garden roses, eucalyptus, centhranthus, and dried rye.

Variegated Roses

Any combination of flowers would look impressive in a strikingly patterned cloisonné vase, but the unique variegated properties of these outstanding roses extends the creative possibilities of this design even further. Each rose boasts two to three colors, and the arrangement spans a broad spectrum ranging from light pink and deep burgundy to yellow, peach, and hot pink to gold, orange, and cream. This mixture forms a stunning palette that is unparalleled during this time of the year.

ELEMENTS

20 garden roses

1 12- by 4-inch vase

DIRECTIONS

Fill the container with water. Clean and condition the roses. Cut and insert the roses one by one into the vase, placing each carefully as if applying brush strokes to a painting. Allow some of the blooms to sit close to the edge of the vase, while others can stand taller.

TRADE SECRET

Tepid water is more effective for conditioning blooms and is absorbed more quickly than cold water.

Autumn Cornucopia

Early autumn orange spray roses, dried amaranthus, orange thistle, and ripe corn are combined in this arrangement displaying nature's abundance. These seemingly incongruous ingredients conspire to create an autumn extravaganza. If any of the elements listed below are not readily available, it should be easy to improvise by scouring local flower shops, vegetable stands, or the backyard for suitable substitutions.

ELEMENTS

24 dried amaranthus blooms

15 orange spray roses

8 orange thistle

12 ears of ripe corn

Floral picks

1 24-inch monkey-branch basket

2 blocks of oasis

2 blocks of Styrofoam

1 large plastic liner

DIRECTIONS

Cut and fit blocks of Styrofoam into the bottom of the container for height. Place the plastic liner on top of the Styrofoam, and cut and fit wet oasis into the plastic liner. Peel the corn husks to expose ripe corn. Cut the corn cobs in half, disposing of the half with the husk. Insert a floral pick into each ear and insert into the oasis. Cut most of the amaranthus, gather it into five groupings, and place the groupings in the oasis randomly. Insert the remaining stems of amaranthus, allowing it to drape and hang naturally. Cut and tuck the spray roses in between the ears of corn and place the orange thistle into the arrangement for height. Make certain to remove any excess foliage or damaged leaves.

Captivating Calla Lilies

This grand arrangement of calla lilies and copper beech is large in scale, but it can be created with ease. The key is the use of bold-shaped elements to establish an impressive form. Here, the large rusty maroon leaves of copper beech epitomize autumn, while the miniature pink calla lilies are showy trumpetlike phantoms that exact elegance. Mixing the two very different components produces a striking balance of unusual shapes pulled together by monochromatic colors.

ELEMENTS

20 miniature pink calla lilies

8 copper beech branches

1 12-inch ice bucket

DIRECTIONS

Fill the bucket with water. Condition and cut the branches so they will sit two feet above the lip of the container. Place the branches into the container, allowing them to roam and wander as they would in nature. Cut and arrange the calla lilies so they are half the height of the branches and reach forward out of the container. This arrangement works best on a pedestal or on an entrance table and should be designed to be viewed on three sides.

TRADE SECRET

Always clean buckets and containers with a mixture of bleach and water before using them to hold fresh flowers. This formula will kill any bacteria and mold. In addition, a few drops of bleach added to the water in an arrangement will act as a preservative and help blooms last longer. Use one quarter of a teaspoon of bleach per gallon of water.

A Spray of Safflowers

A kitchen has plenty of shelves and cupboards that can play host to floral scents and tones. Here, a small kitchen cupboard accommodates cascading sprays of grayish silver eucalyptus and spots of orange safflowers, giving this scene a down-home country feel. Both of these materials can be left in place to dry, creating an everlasting arrangement.

ELEMENTS

100 stems of orange safflowers

1 bunch of eucalyptus branches

DIRECTIONS

Cut and place the branches of eucalyptus, allowing some to stand upright and others to drape in front of the shelf. Cut and insert the safflowers toward the front, evenly distributing the orange buds. Make sure that the branches and buds are settled snugly in place.

TRADE SECRET

Traditionally used by Aborigines as a fever remedy, eucalyptus was also valued for its antiseptic properties and was often added to poultices and applied as a compress to treat wounds or burns. Today, eucalyptus oil is used as a chest rub for colds, bronchitis, and asthma, as well as in compresses for painful joints, inflammations, and burns.

A Burst of Blue Thistle

Blue thistle is one of autumn's treasures. These wildings are perfect by themselves or accompanied by touches of smaller stems, such as the railroad annie used here, which adds a stroke of lively color. These flowers are nestled in an unobtrusive crystal fruit bowl, which provides a beautiful showcase for the thistle.

DIRECTIONS

Cut the wet block of oasis in half and fit it into the bowl. Clean the blue thistle, cutting some of the stems shorter than others so that the back half of the arrangement will be higher than the front. This will add depth to the finished piece. Place the thistle into the oasis. Clean and cut the railroad annie. Insert the stems into the oasis to break up the heavy masses of blue flowers. Fill the container with water and mist.

ELEMENTS

30 blue thistle

25 railroad annie

1 10-inch bowl

1 block of oasis

TRADE SECRET

Always keep an arrangement in a well-lit location (but not in direct sunlight) so that the flowers can continue to grow.

Rustic Baskets of Color

Finding a little bit of paradise in an unexpected place—on a stack of antique books, next to a bowl of fresh fruit, on a kitchen island, or by the window in the corner of a study—can be a delightful discovery. Here, this moss-lined, two-tiered basket successfully adds height, textural variety, and color to an otherwise mundane space. When filled with sun-kissed solidago blooms and crab-apple branches, the baskets take on a delightful form and the entire corner of the room is energized.

ELEMENTS

40 stems of solidago

4 branches of crab apple

Two-tiered basket

Sheet moss, as needed

8 blocks of oasis

DIRECTIONS

Line the baskets with sheet moss, creating a natural receptacle for the flowers. Cut and fit four blocks of wet oasis inside each basket. Line the baskets with the crab-apple branches, fitting them around the oasis blocks and allowing them to peek out randomly from the containers. Clean and cut the solidago stems and insert them into the oasis in both tiers. The flowers on the top tier should stand taller than those on the lower tier, while the lower arrangement should almost touch the bottom of the top basket. Fill with water and mist.

A Pink Splash

Using only one species in a bouquet makes a strong statement. These upright flowering stalks of Monte Casino daisies are a perfect example of this effect as their bright mass of color calls to mind flowers in a perennial border.

ELEMENTS

50 stems of Monte Casino daisies

1 8-inch porcelain vase

DIRECTIONS

Fill the vase with water. Cut and clean away excess and damaged leaves from the stems of the daisies. Cut some stems so they will be almost three times the height of the container, while others can be cut much shorter. Place the taller stems toward the back of the vase, and gradually decrease the flower height as you place stems closer to the front; the center blooms should be half the height of the tallest stems. Some of the shorter blooms can be tucked close to the lip of the vase.

TRADE SECRET

The easiest and cheapest way to keep flowers fresh is to change the water often. It is not necessary to totally change the water every time. Topping it off will do.

A Palette of Yellow and Orange

An arrangement for an end table or coffee table should be designed so it can be viewed from all angles. In addition, the flowers should be short—or cut short—and the arrangement should be small so it won't obstruct conversation or take up space on the table that might be needed to accommodate the occasional magazine or drink glass. Here, this mixture of Golden Fantasie roses and calendula sitting in a round Japanese fishbowl on a cherry side table meets all of these specifications.

ELEMENTS

25 Golden Fantasie roses

15 calendula

1 block of oasis

1 10-inch bowl

DIRECTIONS

Cut and fit the wet oasis inside the bowl. Clean and condition the roses, and begin cutting and placing them around the oasis. The tallest rose should be twice the height of the container; the shortest should be placed just above the edge of the bowl. Turn the container as you arrange the flowers to ensure their even distribution. Cut and clean the calendula and tuck the stems into the oasis in between the roses, interspersing the orange color with the yellow. Do not hesitate to remove and replace stems that seem out of place. Continue to view the arrangement from all angles. When finished, fill the container with water and mist.

Autumn Showstopper

This abundant arrangement of garden roses and red rover daisies graces a dining room table about to be set for an autumn dinner party. This decorative addition has been strategically placed under a glittering crystal chandelier to emphasize the brilliant colors of the season.

ELEMENTS

12 yellow garden roses

12 peach garden roses

12 red rover daisies

12 stems of eucalyptus

2 branches of crab apple

1 14-inch container

2 blocks of oasis

DIRECTIONS

Cut and fit wet blocks of oasis into the container. Clean and condition the roses, and place them into the oasis at focal points. Clean and cut the red rover daisies, and intersperse them throughout the oasis at varying heights. Clean off the lower leaves of the eucalyptus, and insert the stems throughout the arrangement, allowing some to stray downward and others to spike out of the top for height and texture. Clean and cut the crab-apple branches. Place them strategically to fill in openings. Fill the container with water and mist.

TRADE SECRET

For flowers to be able to absorb water, properly prepared oasis must be soaked to the center. The general guideline is to soak a block of oasis in a bucket of water for 10 minutes or until the water bubbles have disappeared.

An Infusion of Color

Letter writing can be a soothing, almost therapeutic process when performed amid a cluster of enchanting blossoms. A rusted bridal basket filled with orange Sensation roses serves as the perfect punctuation mark of color for this old English secretary.

ELEMENTS

9 orange Sensation roses

Dried Spanish moss, as needed

1 basket

DIRECTIONS

Fill the container with water. Clean and condition the roses and place them into the basket so that they form a tight bouquet. Use the Spanish moss to fill in at the bottom of the arrangement. The moss will serve as a soft bed for the roses to sit in.

TRADE SECRET

Try using a variety of locations to display arrangements. Tuck a bouquet into a bookshelf, stand groupings of single stems on a windowsill, or display wandering tulips on a kitchen countertop.

Red Cockscomb

Tall spears of kangaroo paw seem to burst out of clusters of fuzzy red cockscomb in this riveting autumn celebration. Both blooms have unusual shapes, yet they work well together in this creative juxtaposition based on their variation in height. Surrounded by a collection of oriental figurines, this exotic mixture has a far-eastern mood.

ELEMENTS

15 stems of kangaroo paw

10 cockscomb

1 block of oasis

1 12-inch bowl

Dried Spanish moss, as needed

DIRECTIONS

Cut and fit the block of wet oasis into the container. Clean and cut the stems of kangaroo paw so they will be three times the height of the container. Place the kangaroo paw into the oasis in an upright central position. Clean the cockscomb stems, and cut them so they will rest approximately six inches above the edge of the container. Place them into the container so that the kangaroo paw appears to be growing out of a bed created by the cockscomb. Tuck in Spanish moss for a natural finishing touch. Fill the container with water.

TRADE SECRET

To condition cockscomb, dip the stems in boiling water after they have been cut. They should then immediately be placed in buckets of cool water and left to stand undisturbed for several hours.

Golden Elements

Welcome a loved one home from a long day at work with a fresh and invigo-

rating autumn arrangement poised in an entranceway. This seasonal picture

is complete with proud groupings of golden centhranthus and Swedish ivy

in cloisonné containers surrounded by a carpet of Swedish ivy in smaller

cloisonné vases.

ELEMENTS

20 centhranthus

40 Swedish ivy leaves

2 12- to 14-inch vases

3 4- to 6-inch vases

DIRECTIONS

Fill vases with water. Clean and remove excess and damaged leaves from the centhranthus flowers, making certain to remove all leaves that will fall below the water line. Arrange the centhranthus buds and blooms in the taller containers. Tuck individual Swedish ivy leaves close to the lip of the second-tallest container, creating a collar of foliage. Fill two of the smaller containers with Swedish ivy leaves, making sure that the stems of the leaves are immersed in the water. Place one centhranthus bloom in the smallest container.

A Distinctive Combination

This wild garden mixture of pink yarrow and blue monkshood, which is also known as helmet flower, can be adapted to decorate any room. Here, they are placed in an unadorned glass ice bucket so the brightly colored blooms can be showcased.

ELEMENTS

15 blue monkshood

20 pink yarrow

1 10-inch glass container

DIRECTIONS

Fill the container with water. Clean the monkshood and cut most of the stems so they are twice the height of the container. Place these in the container in a fanlike pattern. Clean the yarrow and cut most of the stems so they will be one and a half times the height of the container. Place the yarrow in front of the monkshood. Cut the remaining yarrow stems shorter, and place them toward the front of the arrangement. Remember that this arrangement will be viewed from the front, left, and right sides, and the flowers must be placed accordingly. Take the few remaining stems of monkshood and cut them short. Mix them in with the yarrow to visually break up the hot pink flowers.

CHAPTER FOUR

Winter

Bouquets of warm tones are sure to lift spirits on cold and frosty days. Here is a selection of some of the varieties available throughout the winter months (counterclockwise from bottom right): Tineke roses, white monkshood, cedar branches, hanging amaranthus, Casa Blanca lilies, juniper branches, white campanula, Tineke roses, Casa Blanca lilies, and parrot tulips.

Holiday Table

For a glorious holiday feast on a frosty December night, create a natural tablecovering out of boxwood branches and decorate the greenery with pinecones. Blue and white porcelain vases brimming with peach amaryllis and burgundy roses provide the perfect seasonal focal point. Red roses nestled in the dark green carpet of branches continue the holiday color theme, giving the table depth and creating the illusion of movement.

ELEMENTS

1 bundle of boxwood branches (or any
    branches of shrubbery that lay flat)
50 burgundy roses
20 peach amaryllis
12 pinecones
2 12-inch vases

DIRECTIONS

Purchase and condition roses and amaryllis three to four days before the dinner party to allow them to open to their fullest. On the day of the party, cut three-quarters of the boxwood branches into six-inch sections, removing excess stems at the same time. Wash thoroughly. (Branches can be prepared twenty-four hours ahead by soaking them overnight in a large sink or a bathtub.) Towel-dry leaves and place them on the table. Using the amaryllis and twenty burgundy roses, arrange both centerpieces. Be sure to balance the two colors in the vases, evenly distributing the two flowers because they will be viewed from all angles. Position the finished arrangements on the table. Next, set the table with festive dinner- and flatware. To add the boxwood, place generous amounts in one layer directly onto the table, leaving minimum openings. Fill in any openings with pinecones to emphasize the naturalness of the setting. Scatter color around the table with closely cropped burgundy roses.

Dessert Bouquet

A burst of hot pink roses gathered in a sterling silver teapot serves as a focal

point on this dessert table. The sweet colors of the flowers complement the

white chocolate and gold-leaf jewel-box cake, petit fours, and strawberries.

For a touch of greenery, lemon leaf dusted with confectioners' sugar borders

a mocha yule log. Lining the plates of petit fours with rose petals not only

adds color but also provides an unexpected finishing touch.

ELEMENTS

40 to 50 Galaxy hot pink roses

1 12-inch container

DIRECTIONS

Purchase and condition roses two to three days before the party to allow them to open to their fullest. The day you make the arrangement, trim the stems so the blooms will remain six to eight inches above the lip of the container you choose. Fill the container with water, and add the roses one by one, saving a few to use only for their petals. When creating the arrangement, spotlight the most beautiful bloom by giving it a central position. When placing the roses, also make sure that open blossoms are visible from all sides.

Gently pull the outer petals from the bases of the remaining roses, discarding the centers. Use the fullest petals to decorate the table.

Hanging Amaranthus

With a fluid elegance that is both unaffected and elaborate, hanging amaranthus lends an air of grace and distinction to this living room. Trailing down a decoupaged Botticelli container, these amaranthus stems set the mood for an intimate mid-winter get-together with friends.

TRADE SECRET

This is the time of the year to plant a tree—one for yourself and perhaps one for a friend. Flowering fruit trees make wonderful gifts. Try a cherry for pink blossoms or a Bradford pear for white.

ELEMENTS

50 stems of hanging amaranthus

1 10-inch container or cylinder vase

Fresh Spanish moss

DIRECTIONS

Fill the container with water. Cut and clean each amaranthus stem, making certain that no leaves will fall below the water line. Insert the stems one by one, allowing the foliage to drape and weave. Tuck Spanish moss into the bottom of the arrangement to hold the stems together.

A Lofty Trio

This trio of winter delights settled on a bed of fragrant cedar branches adds warmth and relaxed beauty to this white-on-white setting. The campanula and monkshood add two more variations on the white theme while the deep hues of the ruby amaranthus contribute a richness. The iron containers on this glass coffee table have been softened by tufts of Spanish moss.

ELEMENTS

30 white campanula

25 white monkshood

4 stems of amaranthus

6 cedar branches

3 6-inch containers

3 blocks of oasis

Spanish moss, as needed

TRADE SECRET

Long-stemmed flowers such as monkshood can be cut and used in smaller, shorter pieces, ensuring that no part of the flower is wasted.

DIRECTIONS

Cut and fit the wet oasis into each of the containers. Clean and condition the campanula and monkshood. Cut two-thirds of the campanula so it is one and a half times the height of the container; two-thirds of the monkshood should be cut to twice the height of the container. Cut the remaining third of both flowers shorter to add depth. Insert the two types of flowers into two separate containers, placing the shorter stems toward the front. Clean and condition the amaranthus, and place it into the oasis so that the height equals that of the taller monkshood. Allow a few stems to drape over the side for a more natural effect. Tuck the Spanish moss around the edges of all of the arrangements. Set the three finished pieces on the table where they will be displayed, positioning the shorter campanula arrangement in front of the taller monkshood. Lay the cedar branches flat on the table, tucking the woody stems in between the three pots.

Piano Vignette

This unexpected marriage of flowers, vegetables, and verdant grass blends easily with the eclectic collection of instruments and art objects found in this dramatically lit room. The gnarly twig basket filled with peach and red roses, mushrooms, and asparagus relaxes the formality of the room, while the blades of grass stand tall in the moss-covered crate, making light of the dark walls. The sterling silver candelabra adds to the sense of drama and increases the height of the still-life setting as it rises above the flowers. A piano shawl draped cavalierly on top of the black mahogany piano acts as a backdrop, holding the separate elements together as well as protecting the hardwood surface.

TRADE SECRET

Although crates filled with grass can easily be purchased, it can be fun to grow your own. Start by filling a crate with potting soil. Sprinkle the soil with grass seeds (line the crate with plastic if using wood), place in a sunlit window, and keep moist. Approximately five to six days later, tender young blades of grass will appear.

ELEMENTS

20 burgundy roses

30 peach Osiana roses

20 white-cap mushrooms

12 spears of asparagus

Sheet moss, as needed

1 16-inch basket

4 blocks of oasis

1 plastic liner

32 wood picks

DIRECTIONS

Purchase and condition roses two to three days in advance to allow them to open to their fullest. Line the basket with a plastic liner. Cut wet blocks of oasis to size, and push them inside the basket vertically, making sure they fit tightly and the height of the oasis blocks is about eight inches above the top of the basket. Insert a wood pick halfway into the side of each asparagus and mushroom, and place the vegetables into the blocks of oasis on an angle. After half the vegetables have been inserted, cut the rose stems so that when they are added to the bouquet they will not protrude any farther than the mushrooms. Distribute the rose colors evenly throughout the oasis. Finish the arrangement by inserting the remaining vegetables and tucking moistened sheet moss into any openings. Fill the container with water to sustain the bouquet.

Sophisticated Roses

Presented in aged porcelain cachepots, these identical white rose bouquets add a delicate, feminine, almost dreamy quality to this dining room setting. A longstanding favorite, single-color rose bouquets create a distinctively old-fashioned ambiance.

ELEMENTS

50 Tineke roses

2 8-inch cachepots

2 blocks of oasis

DIRECTIONS

Fit one block of wet oasis into each cachepot. Clean off the thorns and condition all the roses. Cut the stems on an angle with a sharp knife and insert them randomly into the oasis. Try to work on both arrangements at the same time; this helps to keep the design and shape similar.

TRADE SECRET

If rose blooms begin to wilt before you've had a chance to use them, try placing them in a tub of cool water overnight, making sure they are totally submerged.

Parrot Tulips

Brimming with vivacious parrot tulips cushioned by scented juniper branches,

this genial arrangement is sure to lift spirits out of the mid-winter doldrums.

ELEMENTS

40 parrot tulips

2 juniper branches

1 cachepot with a 5-inch opening

DIRECTIONS

Fill the cachepot with four inches of water. Condition the juniper branches by smashing the woody stems, and clean off any greenery that will fall below the water line. Place the bed of branches into the water. Cut and clean tulips, removing much of the foliage so that the flowers will fit into the opening of the container. Place the tulips into the cachepot, allowing them to stretch and roam.

TRADE SECRET

To straighten tulip stems before you begin arranging, place the tulips inside a newspaper. Roll the paper up around them, and plunge the bundle into cool water. This should do the trick.

A Touch of Color

Adding a splash of color in an otherwise sparely decorated room invokes an air of festivity and good cheer. Here, in a foyer, hot pink Galaxy and peach Osiana roses settled on a charming turn-of-the-century carved wooden shelf extend a warm welcome to arriving dinner guests. For this winter's eve dinner party, these two colors were grouped together to allow the lighter roses to act as an accent for the darker roses.

TRADE SECRET

When selecting flowers to decorate various rooms throughout a home, one option is to create an overall theme by choosing the same flower, such as roses or tulips, in different colors.

ELEMENTS

20 to 30 hot pink Galaxy roses

10 peach Osiana roses

3 stems of lemon leaf

DIRECTIONS

Purchase roses two to three days prior to creating this arrangement. At that time, condition each rose and place them in bacteria-free, clean buckets of lukewarm water, which will ensure that they achieve their fullest bloom. On the day of the party, place the roses on top of the shelf one by one to form a splendidly layered bouquet of color, cutting the stems short and tucking them in so they will not be visible from any of the vantage points throughout the room. Finish the arrangement by tucking in a few stems of lemon leaf at the bottom edges. Mist.

A Bountiful Kitchen

When a trip to the fresh market produces a bounty such as this, why hide it in the vegetable crisper? To give guests a tantalizing view of what's to be served later that evening, line the kitchen sink with sheet moss and create an appetizing display such as this. The various shades of green are enhanced by layering light on top of dark—artichokes, asparagus, Portobello mushrooms, broccoli, white-cap mushrooms, and kale. After guests have taken the grand tour of the house, the arrangement can be easily dismantled and cleaned as preparations for dinner begin. Fully popped red roses nestled cozily with citrus in a wood crate add visual punch and color to the winter sonata of vegetables.

TRADE SECRET

It's a good idea to cut all flowers on an angle. This will create a point at the end of the stems, facilitating their placement in the oasis and allowing water to easily feed the blooms.

ELEMENTS

24 Galaxy pink and red Lady Liberty
  roses

3 oranges

1 18-inch wood container

Sheet moss

2 blocks of oasis

1 plastic liner

DIRECTIONS

Condition flowers two to three days before the event to allow them to open to their fullest. On the day of the party, line the container with the plastic. Cut the oasis, and press it inside the crate. Place and arrange the oranges in the box. Cut the rose stems down to four inches, varying the heights slightly to add depth. Place in the oasis. Add water. Tuck sheet moss around the edges of the container to hide the oasis.

115

Fragrant Lilies

A lofty spray of deep burgundy amaranthus stems serves as a dramatic backdrop for these aromatic white lilies. With such remarkable blooms, lilies are best when showcased in a simple, unpretentious grouping.

ELEMENTS

6 Casa Blanca lilies or white maintain lilies

12 stems of amaranthus

2 branches of juniper berry

3 low 6- to 8-inch containers

TRADE SECRET

Lily pollen will stain almost anything it comes in contact with: other flowers, linens, clothing, and skin. Therefore, make certain to remove the pollen from the lilies before trying to arrange them. To remove the pollen, hold the stem firmly with one hand while gently pulling the pollen off with the other. If a bloom has been stained by pollen, it can be cleaned by gently wiping the inside with a small piece of foam rubber. This material can be purchased at most fabric stores.

DIRECTIONS

Fill the containers with water. Clean and cut the lilies. Cut four at varying heights to fill the larger vase, and trim the other two close to the bloom for the shortest container. Cut and condition the juniper berry branches and add them to the arrangements as accents or where needed for support. Cut and place the amaranthus into the tallest container and place it behind the lily groupings.

A Rose Collection

While a single rose in a vase might get lost in its surroundings, a grouping of vases each filled with an individual bloom makes a spirited, dramatic collaboration. Any collection of bottles or vases would be appropriate; here, a collection of glass bottles are positioned on an end table to catch and reflect the available light.

ELEMENTS

12 to 24 burgundy roses

7 to 12 containers

DIRECTIONS

Clean the roses so there are no leaves left below the water line (this will prevent the water from taking on an unpleasant odor). Cut the rose stems on an angle at varying heights as you place the flowers individually into the water-filled containers. Experiment with varying heights, leaving some flower heads just above the lips of the vases and others three to six inches above.

TRADE SECRET

Collections of many types can be used as temporary homes for buds. Those you may choose to consider include pitchers, tea cups, silver goblets, and cruets.

WINTER
WEEK TWELVE

Lily-of-the-Valley

The gentle, pastoral combination of lily-of-the-valley and seeded grass

sprouting in a container wrapped in coconut bark brings a soft and fragrant

whisper of nature indoors.

ELEMENTS

50 lily-of-the-valley bulbs

1 small box of grass seed

1 bag of potting soil

Coconut bark, as needed

Raffia, as needed

1 12-inch flowerpot

DIRECTIONS

Approximately two weeks before you want to display this arrangement, plant the lily-of-the-valley bulbs in the container. Wrap the container in coconut bark, tying it on with raffia. Place in a sunny, warm spot, and water and mist regularly. A week later, after the bulbs have sprouted, sprinkle the container with grass seed. In about five or six more days, the grass will have sprouted and the bulbs will have blooms.

Highlighting With Hyacinths

The lovely simplicity of an arrangement can be amplified when positioned below a magnificent mirror. In this arrangement, a cluster of lily-of-the-valley placed directly into the center of a bouquet of hyacinths brings out the various shades of blue and adds depth and dimension to the composition. A cut-crystal container takes full advantage of the dramatic lighting and the mirror's reflecting properties.

ELEMENTS

25 purple hyacinths

20 lily-of-the-valley

Sheet moss, as needed

1 6-inch bucket or container

DIRECTIONS

Cut all hyacinths to the same length and place them in the container. Trim the lily-of-the-valley stems only slightly, allowing them enough length to reach the water. Group the lily-of-the-valley in your hand, creating a bouquet, and place them in the center of the hyacinths. Place dampened sheet moss into the sides of the container, forcing the hyacinths to stand upright.

TRADE SECRET

Designed to force fragrant bulbs, decorative English hyacinth glasses bring springtime cheer in the middle of winter. The mouths of these containers are wide enough to hold one bulb, and the long, narrow neck and flared bottom are designed to hold a generous amount of water. Glasses are available in many colors and can be purchased inexpensively at your local florist's shop. Many older glasses are considered collectibles and can be found in antique stores or flea markets.

Appendix

CLEANING & CONDITIONING

When cut flowers fade quickly, wilt, or look sickly, it is often because they were not properly conditioned. Cut flowers will last longer if they are treated correctly from the moment they are harvested. Conditioning flowers is well worth the initial investment of time; in fact, the more time spent, the longer the blooms will perform. So, follow these simple rules and reap the rewards.

1. Always cut flower stems on an angle with a sharp knife. Do not use scissors, because they squeeze the stem closed and delay the intake of water. Plunge the cut stems into water immediately. This will inhibit the stems from closing and will allow them to drink water at once. Some branches and buds should be left to drink for a few days to allow them to open fully before arranging. In any case, when it is time to make the arrangement, always make a fresh new cut prior to inserting the stems into the oasis or container where they will be displayed.

2. For flowers with thicker, less fleshy stems, such as a rose, it is best to scrape the tough stem to open up a larger area for absorbing water. For woody stems such as lilac, thinner rhododendron branches, and forsythia, it is important to not only scrape the bark but also to make a vertical cut, a few inches long, up the center of the branch.

3. When the bark is very thick, such as magnolia, crab apple, camellia, beech, or cedar, help these stems drink by smashing the ends with a hammer or mallet. Afterward, make a three-quarter-inch cut up the center of the stem to expose even more surface for water absorption.

4. Some stems ooze a milky fluid after they are cut. These should be cauterized to prevent the vital fluids from escaping. This can be done by dipping the stalk into boiling water for a few seconds or placing the stem directly into a flame or a lit match for a moment. This clears out the passage for better water absorption. Immediately place the stems into buckets of lukewarm water.

5. Hollow stems, such as lupines and delphiniums, need to be literally filled with water in order for this life-sustaining substance to reach the bloom. To accomplish this, hold the stem upside down and pour water into it. Place your thumb over the end, and turn the flower right side up while simultaneously placing it into the water-filled container where the arrangement will be made.

6. Always remove all foliage that will fall below the water line so that the water will remain clean and bacteria-free. For roses, it is best to trim off the thorns for easier handling and arranging.

7. Pinch away any excess blooms that have faded or wilted to encourage healthy new ones to open.

Index